How to Stand in the Midst of Rejection

How to Stand in the Midst of Rejection
Copyright © 2024 Gloria Duff.

Softcover ISBN: 978-1-950880-04-1
eBook ISBN: 978-1-950880-05-8

All rights reserved. No part of this publication may be reproduced, distributed, or transmitted in any form or by any means, including photocopying, recording, or other electronic or mechanical methods, without the prior written permission of the publisher, except in the case of brief quotations embodied in critical reviews and certain other noncommercial uses permitted by copyright law. For permission requests, write to the publisher, addressed "Attention: Permissions Coordinator," at the address below.

THE HOLY BIBLE, NEW INTERNATIONAL VERSION®, NIV® Copyright © 1973, 1978, 1984, 2011 by Biblica, Inc.® Used by permission. All rights reserved worldwide.
Scripture taken from the New King James Version®. Copyright © 1982 by Thomas Nelson. Used by permission. All rights reserved.

Any references to historical events, real people, or real places are used fictitiously. Names, characters, and places are products of the author's imagination.

Graphic Designer: Pastor Erlene Taylor

"This is an excellent read on how to process and work through rejection and forgiveness. It is obvious from Gloria's testimony that you can't be free from anything without forgiveness. She does an excellent job to bring these truths home in a concise and easy to understand way. This book will bring freedom to those who are in a true relationship with Jesus as they read and apply these things on a daily basis in their journey with Him!"

– Dr. Sherill Piscopo,
Evangel Association of Churches & Ministries

"I have known Gloria for about sixteen years. I have seen her pain, her hurts and her rejection. On the other hand, I have seen God at work in her life doing great things. Little did we know God was doing a great work. The metamorphosis of God unfolded in her life as a result. I was abundantly blessed by this book. It was my rescue and recovery. Allow this book to minister to you too."

– Rev. Patricia Hampton, aka Puppet Preacher

"As I journeyed through each chapter of this book, it was a constant reminder of God's loves for the brokenhearted and rejected people, and for all who have faced crises in their lives. Elder Gloria Duff, through her series of events, shows us a God who teaches us how to forgive as He heals and delivers us from ours past hurts and our struggle through the pain. This book will give you some tools to help you overcome any obstacle you may be going through due to rejection."

– Your sister in Christ,
Minister Janis Moore

"Who could have imagined my 'neighbor' (Elder Gloria), who moved in next door to me several years ago, was carrying deep within her innermost being God's pathway to freedom from the pain of rejection—waiting for His appointed time to be released for the Body of Christ. Now is the time! Now is the time to deal with it—God's way. My neighbor has walked the sometimes-painful path, suffered and, like Jesus, has overcome!

This book guides you along the path, should you choose to take it, from pain to power, from hurt to healing, from denied to delivered, from bondage to freedom, and from rejection to revival. Enjoy the journey!"

– Pastor Erlene Taylor

"In this book, Gloria, guided by the Holy Spirit, leads us beautifully through the process of healing from the spirit of rejection. She shares her healing journey in a manner that is a testimony to God and a blessing to others.

When reading this book, I reflected upon the pain of my own journeys and upon the joy of completing those journeys by entering into a closer relationship with God. It also gave me another confirmation that God's Word is true and will never fall short of His promises.

This book will guide you in facilitating your own healing of the heart, spirit, mind, and soul. Allow it to guide you to your place of hurt, examine it, and let God heal you. Your healing will be a testimony of God's healing power and a blessing to others."

– Mary Mixon,
Your Spiritual Godmother

How to Stand in the Midst of Rejection

Gloria Duff

This book is dedicated to the late Bishop Jerry Piscopo, my father-in-the faith.

FOREWORD

I am honored to write the foreword to this power packed book, *How to Stand In the Midst of Rejection* by my friend, Gloria G. Duff. I have known Gloria for several years, and I'm so blessed that the Holy Spirit divinely connected us years ago through a shared desire to attend a prayer conference, and we have been connected since that day. Gloria's passion for prayer and intercession has helped her birthed this book, and I'm so blessed to have been able to journey alongside her to witness a promise being fulfilled in her life by "Abba Father."

When she first mentioned this book to me years ago, I could see then how the Holy Spirit was preparing her to be healed from the spirit of rejection so she could write from a healed place instead of a bitter place.

The spirit of rejection does not care what you know; its strength is in what and how it makes you feel and what you accept as truth. Gloria shares many times in this book the importance of forgiveness and how she allowed the Holy Spirit to heal her emotionally and spiritually. After many draft revisions, she now powerfully shares how you, too, can be healed from rejection. I'm sure all who read this book will be blessed, just as I was, and it will prove even more beneficial as the Holy Spirit brings illumination to each reader personally.

In closing, I pray that this book will be the catalyst

for healing and deliverance to everyone who reads it. It can also be a shared resource to help someone that's dealing with rejection; they too can stand in the midst of rejection and be brought to wholeness.

Dr. Sharon Smith

Evangel Association of Churches and Ministries

Heart to Heart Ministries

Acknowledgements

- I would like to thank Jesus, my Lord and Savior, and the Holy Spirit, for leading and guiding me to write this book.
- I thank my pastors, the late Bishop Jerry Piscopo and my senior pastor, Dr. Sherill Piscopo, Evangel Christian Church, for believing in me. They directed me to their publisher, Pastors Simon and Trish Presland, to whom I am so grateful.
- One of my best friends and prayer partner, Reverend Patricia Hampton (the puppet preacher), who constantly kept telling me, "Duff I need you to finish that book."
- Pastor Erlene Taylor; when I mentioned my book to her and told her a little about it, she designed the cover.
- One of my best friends, mentor, sister, prayer partner, 'ride or live' partner, Dr. Sharon Smith, who has journeyed with me in this walk.
- Bishop Michael Jones and Pastor Brenda Jones, Fountain of Truth Christian Center, who helped raise me up to be the woman of God I am by showing me that I needed to pray and read the Word. As an intercessor, they permitted me to cover their

ministry in prayer. When they saw the calling on my life, they licensed me as a Minister of the Gospel and later ordained me as an Elder.
- The many teachings from my spiritual Godmother, Mary B. Mixon. You have been my support every step of the way. Thank you for being a mentor, friend, motherly adviser, and most of all loving me and my family.
- My children, DeAndre Javon, Claude LeVar, Tiffany Michelle, and Steven Martez, whom I thank God for. When things got hard, you gave me a reason to keep going through your encouragement and input ... I love you!
- Mother Estelle Cohen, who helped raise me up as an intercessor through her teaching on faith.
- Bishop William Murphy, for all the prayer conferences I have been attending every year.
- Prophetess Catrina Butts, you have been an encourager, and I'll always remember you praying for my lungs when we first met. You also encouraged me to finish this book!
- Thanks to my friend and publisher, Simon Presland, for encouraging and working with me to complete this book ... and never giving up on me!
- To *all* who had a hand in my growing and maturing in my calling as an intercessor, thank you!
- Finally, to my Heavenly Father and the Holy Spirit, you are my light and my love, and to Jesus, you are the joy of my salvation!

Gloria Duff

My Prayer Journey

My prayer ministry began after the loss of my mother, Mary M. Hunter-Bogan, on September 26, 1984. I grieved for a whole year, cried myself to sleep, and was angry with God for taking my mom, who was my best friend.

She sometimes stood in the spot that my father should have. Along with the Lord, my mom raised seven children (we call ourselves "the magnificent seven") all of whom graduated from high school and have gone further. Four boys and three girls, I am the oldest girl, so I had to be a helper to my mom. But it wasn't until I realized I couldn't cry anymore or hurt any more that I began to pray.

My mother and I were going to bury my grandmother on my dad's side, who had passed away two days before my mom. When we were traveling to Montgomery, Alabama, my mom passed on the Greyhound bus. I thought my world had been turned upside down that day because she was with me trying to support me.

I took on the guilt of not bringing her back to my siblings, not knowing how to call and tell them what had happened and which one of them to call. The mayor of Montgomery wanted to keep her there because she and her family were well known and to have a memorial service. But, I just wanted to get back where someone felt what I felt. After a year of grieving, I turned to prayer, asking God, "Why did you take me miles away from my home and my loved ones, and why did You take my mother?"

She and I did not always see eye to eye because there were some things we had to forgive each other for, but we talked every day. Matter of fact, I tell people I had three names, Gloria, Barbara, and "Heffa" when I didn't call her before she called me. God said that the reason I was the one with my mom when she passed away was because I was the strong one; my brothers were mama's boys, and my sisters would not have been able to deal with it the way I did.

It resulted in me praying and asking God not to take the good memories of my mother from me. However, the day she passed away, I watched them take her off the bus in a black bag, and I wanted it erased from my memory. So, I prayed and prayed because my mother was a praying woman. Her prayers were so unselfish. She would always pray, "God, I am not asking you for anything. I thank you for what you have already done, and before I leave this world, allow me to see my children grow into adulthood. I don't want to be a burden to my children."

She passed away, giving the prayer mantle to me. She said that she had made it with seven children and I could make it with four. I was five months pregnant with my youngest son, and already had two boys and a girl.

I went to her grave site one time and relived that day, with God telling me as the angel told Mary and the others at the tomb after the crucifixion in Matthew 28:2, that just as Jesus was not there, your mother was not there. But she was with the Lord. From that day I began praying more for others than myself, repenting and asking for forgiveness for being angry with God for taking my mom. I began to realize that we all had an appointed time to be here on earth and that her work was finished. As a God fearing, Holy Ghost filled single parent, raising seven children to graduate from high school and go further, this was a miracle from God.

After my mom's death I was led to the Fountain of Truth Christian Center, where I joined the intercessor team because of my passion to pray. Under the leadership of Bishop Michael and Brenda Jones, after a couple of years of learning, God impressed upon my pastors to place me as lead over S.W.A.T. (Spiritual Warriors Assignment Team). For several years, I would take the intercessors to Chene Park in Detroit, Michigan, once a year.

One night I was awakened by the Holy Spirit. I was having labor pains, with God telling me, "Now that you have given birth to your prayer ministry, the placenta has to come, which will be called 100 Men and Woman at the Water." My first assignment and mission were to call men and women to the water, praising, worshiping, and praying together. By doing so, the people would be healed, delivered, and set free. People have received salvation and healing, and those who have strayed away from the faith have now returned. There have been people that received the infilling of the Holy Ghost with the evidence of speaking in tongues. We had a foot washing one year, and we have given out book bags every year. The ministry had grown larger each year. People stop and join us, asking for prayer and we feed everyone who wants to eat. God promised that because I honored my assignment in 2018, the year I lost my grandson, that He would double everything each year and He has been faithful in providing.

I now reside under the leadership of the late Dr. Jerry Piscopo and current senior pastor, Dr. Sherill Piscopo at Evangel Christian Church, in Roseville, Michigan. I am on the Wednesday night intercessor team and a part of Friday Night Hour of Power Prayer Team, and Monday Lunch Hour

Seekers. On Tuesday and Thursday morning, I lead the prayer for the nation and covering of the House of God and His people. Every year in August, we meet at a local park on the third or fourth Saturday.

After fasting and praying at The Sanctuary in White Water, Wisconsin, the Holy Spirit impressed upon me to take the limits off of God, and to change the name from "100 Men and Women at the Water" to "Gathering of the Intercessors". People continued to be healed, delivered, and set free as God does the work. My team and I are vehicle who God uses, because of our passion to pray and to see the people of God blessed. I am also part of the Triumph Warriors Prayer Team and other prayer ministries. I taught on prayer in Christian Education at the Fountain of Truth Christian Education Week under the leadership of Bishop Michael Jones. I have also taught in the Baptist Christian Education Week in Southwest Detroit, under the leadership of the late Pastor Steve Lee.

Introduction

You may be wondering why I wrote this book! Well, the truth is this was not my idea; I was inspired by the Holy Spirit to write what you are about to read.

Back in 2010, I was sound asleep one night when God woke me up at 2 a.m. He said to me, "The reason why you went through so much rejection was not to harm you but to help you. As you help others overcome their rejection through the book you will write, I will heal you as well."

I said, "Book, Lord? What book?"

That's when he gave me the name of the book you are holding in your hands. *How to Stand in the Midst of Rejection* was written for me and you, so that you don't have to succumb to the sad and bad feelings you've struggled with for way too long. Rejection isn't your portion in life! God sent Jesus to take your place.

Think about this ... the Bible says of Jesus, "Who has believed our message and to whom has the arm of the Lord been revealed? He grew up before him like a tender shoot, and like a root out of dry ground. He had no beauty or majesty to attract us to him, nothing in his appearance that we should desire him. He was despised and rejected by mankind, a man of suffering, and familiar with pain. Like one from whom people hide their faces he was despised, and we held him in low esteem" (Isaiah 53:1-3, NIV). So we see that Jesus suffered rejection from everyone.

Why, then, do I say that he took your place of rejection? Isaiah 53:4-6 (NIV) tells us, "Surely he took up our pain and bore our suffering, yet we considered him punished by God, stricken by him, and afflicted. But he was pierced for our transgressions, he was crushed for our iniquities; the punishment that brought us peace was on him, and by his wounds we are healed. We all, like sheep, have gone astray, each of us has turned to our own way; and the Lord has laid on him the iniquity of us all." Jesus took upon himself all of your suffering, all of your rejection, all of your hurts and wounds. He knows what you've gone through, and has willingly taken upon himself all of your pain.

How do I know this? Jesus plainly tells us that, "The Spirit of the Lord is on me, because he has anointed me to proclaim good news to the poor. He has sent me to proclaim freedom for the prisoners and recovery of sight for the blind, to set the oppressed free, to proclaim the year of the Lord's favor" (Luke 4:18-19, NIV). Jesus wants to set you free! He wants to heal your heart and shower you with God's favor.

As you read this book, God will do for you exactly what he has done for me—I am free from rejection and I live a life full of God's favor. And you can too! God doesn't show favoritism (see Acts 10:34); what he has done for me he will do for you as well.

I trust this book will bless you and will draw you to a place where you can fully trust God; a place where you can receive your healing from rejection, and be free to be the person God has designed you to be!

God's favor is shining upon you!
Rev. Gloria G. Duff
EACM member
Gloria G. Duff Ministries

Prologue

A Word from the Lord

I received a word from the Lord concerning this book: "Wherefore, my beloved brethren, let every man be swift to hear, slow to speak, slow to wrath: For the wrath of man worketh not the righteousness of God (James 1:19-20, KJV). My people need to hear your story and as they read and meditate on this book they too will be healed, delivered and set free. The body of Christ is hurting and I have given you some of the keys to ease the pain. My daughter, will you allow me to heal my people through what I have given you?

"The enemy desires you be shredded like wheat, but I have prayed for you. You will walk in the destiny and purpose that I have ordained for you to walk in. My daughter, get ready, this is your season. Walk in it. Watch, pray, and obey, and I will show the evidence of your prayers. The effective, fervent prayer of a righteous person avails much (James 5:16). So, stand still and see the salvation of the Lord. I know the thoughts that I have towards you, says the Lord, thoughts of peace and not of evil to give an expected end" (Jeremiah 29:11).

Chapter 1

The Beginning of Rejection

The rejection I suffered started when I was a young girl raised in the south, living in the country. I was known as Gloria Glisteen Bogan, aka, Barbara Bogan. My aunt wanted me to be named Barbara, but my mother wanted the name that she gave me—Gloria. My aunt insisted on calling me Barbara with my entire family and close friends, and Barbara was the name I had to explain all my life. It was so annoying.

I was born in Montgomery, AL, January 6, 1957. My dad left my mom when I was young, so I never really knew him, and certainly didn't know of his love for me. I do remember my dad coming around occasionally, but when he did, I hid! I was ashamed of him because I knew he was a gambler and he didn't like to work. I lived in Montgomery until age 11. I didn't lack for food or clothing—my grandfather, whom I called "Dad," was a farmer and helped take care of many. My mother took really good care of her children, but I always felt empty inside; I had a "dad-sized" hole in my heart. I knew nothing about a real father's love, a natural father, that is.

After the Detroit riots of 1968, my mother moved us

to Michigan. I was the oldest girl out of seven children—four brothers, myself and my two younger sisters.

I received Jesus Christ at an early age and was baptized in water. We had to walk miles to get to church and by the time we got there we had to clean our shoes with leaves because they were so muddy after walking through the woods. I did not really understand salvation; all I knew was that there was something different about me.

As I look back over my life, I can see God's favor even before I knew Him. I remember my first day of school in Lowndes County, Alabama. My oldest brother had the pleasure of taking me at the age of six to Hicks Hill Elementary where there were six different grades in one room. We each had our corners, and I was so excited my first day. My brother fed me big wheel cookies all day and I felt spoiled.

While I was happy at school and at home most of the time, whenever my father came around, the emptiness I had in my heart would always return. Being the type of person he was, my siblings and family would tease me. Why, you may ask? I was my father's only child, and I was always told, "You're just like your dad." Those words made me angry. My father would waste his money, then come home and take my mom's. Whenever he came around, I would hide from him and my siblings so I would not have to endure the shame of knowing he was my father.

Chapter 2

Rejection in the Family

We came from a middle-class family. My grandfather had a farm where we raised cows, horses, hogs, chickens, goats, and other animals. We also had a cotton field, sugar cane, a syrup mill, and a corn mill. We had a garden where we grew all types of vegetables such as sweet potatoes, cucumber, peanuts, corn, watermelon, peas, okra, and cantaloupe.

I grew up with mostly boys. I was the oldest girl born in between three boys and surrounded by uncles and aunts who were not my age. The boys rejected me because they didn't think girls should do certain things or go certain places. I felt left out and alone. I insisted on doing some things they dared me not to do and go places I was forbidden to go. When my brothers climbed a tree, I did too. When they made horses out of corn stalks, I did too. They made up a game where you rolled tractor tires at each other, and if you get knocked down, oh well. I played too!

I was courageous, strong and determined to fit in with the boys and prove to them that I could do everything they could, if not more. Although I still felt unwanted, I did my best to fit in and be a part of what they were doing.

My mother left me and some of my siblings with our grandparents for two years in 1966, while she and my oldest brother and baby sister headed to Detroit to find housing for the rest of the family. Even though we were taken care of, we were sometimes not treated right. My grandfather was not around much of the time, due to farming and being a musician, and we were left with relatives who would sometimes mistreat us.

My siblings and I received what we did not deserve. My oldest brother got beaten so bad once that we had to put Salt Pork on him to heal. I received a whipping for not doing other people's chores and telling the truth about it. I was made to admit to something I didn't do.

We were fed but treated cruelly. At times, we got whipped for just standing around while others got chastised. There were times I received a whipping for wetting the bed, even though I didn't do it.

Now that I'm an adult, God has shown me that if I can forgive my relatives, he can "reveal to heal" and I can move on with my life. I cannot do this on my own, but, "I can do all things through Christ who strengthens me" (Philippians 4:19, NIV). Only God can heal such a deep internal wound.

For some reason my older brother and I just could not see eye to eye. We clashed for whatever reason. It was as if he despised me for being born. I've also felt rejected by some of my siblings throughout of my life. Maybe I was, shall I say, the black sheep of the family?

My nose seemed to always bother people; it was always at the center of attention. My family would call me names like Big Nose, Wide Nose, and Flat Nose. I did not know Scripture or what God had to say about who I am, so their comments gave me a complex about my nose.

I had long, black wavy hair like my paternal grandmother on my dad's side, who was part Indian. One year, I had the measles and was given a bath by my grandmother against my mother's instructions. Sores broke out all over my body causing me to go to the hospital. The doctor had to shave my head and after that my family started teasing me, calling me Baldhead and Onion Head. This created anger in me, feelings of rejection, and wanting to fight back. I felt that everyone was against me.

At that time, I was in bondage to what people thought. People said mean things and I took their words at face value. Matthew 12:34, NIV, says, "You brood of vipers, how can you who are evil say anything good? For the mouth speaks what the heart is full of." This tells me that those who were mean to me had hatred in their hearts towards me.

Even though my family was mean to me at times, I still loved them. And as an adult, I could not simply walk away from them. The Bible tells us that Jesus was around all kinds of people, and he walked with people who denied and betrayed Him. He tells us that we are to "love our neighbors" and to "pray for those who persecute you" (Matthew 5:44, NIV). The Bible tells us that we are to love our neighbor as ourselves and to love one another as God has loved us. This is a challenging task but you can do this and it does work. Be careful what seeds you sow. When you sow seeds of evil or unkindness, they are sure to return to you and sometimes worse. I also had to deal with the insult of being made to feel less than who I was, being called a loser and told, "I'm sick of you."

If you've been in this position or a similar situation, right now you need to stand up and rebuke any negative statements and word curses spoken over you, your children, and/or your family. I've had to do this many times. I've had to denounce every word curse and send it back to the dry places. Even to this day, I continue to bind and loose any negativity over my life. As Jesus said, "whatever you bind on earth will be bound in heaven, and whatever you loose on earth will be loosed in heaven" (Matthew 16:18; 18:18, NIV). Repeat after me: "I declare and decree that I am not a loser nor are my children. We are the head and not the tail. We are above and not beneath. We are heirs of God and joint heirs with Jesus. We are more than conquerors through Jesus Christ who loves us. We are the lenders and not the borrowers; our needs are met without debt; we are healthy and wealthy and walking in prosperity."

Now you might think that's how the story ends. But there was a season when I was rejected by some of my children and grandchildren. It hurt and was devastating. However, I reminded myself that they were holding onto bitterness, resentment, unforgiveness, anger, strife, and coldness that had been sown into their hearts by the Adversary. Some of my children wouldn't answer their phone when I called. Hurtful words were spoken and sent my way. How great a love a mother has for her children, a closeness she longs for and desires from them!

What did I do with the hurt that I carried inside so deeply? I could only carry it to God. The more I tried to do it on my own, the worse became.

There were times when my family became negative and critical when it came to my gift of intercession. They didn't want to hear my prayers unless it pertained to them, and that hurt me to my heart.

But, "Thanks be to God, who delivers me through Jesus Christ our Lord!" (Romans 7:25, NIV). God has brought reconciliation and healing in my family. As 3 John 2 says that above all things, He wishes for us to prosper and be in health even, as our soul prospers.

My family will be made whole and I will not let them hinder me another day. I refuse to lie by the Pool of Bethesda. I remind myself that, "Therefore, if anyone is in Christ, the new creation has come: The old has gone, the new is here!" (2 Corinthians, 5:17 NIV). I'm going to get my *complete* healing. I will not be made to feel like I'm less than what God says I am.

Yes, there are times when I want to give up. I long for my family to see me the way God sees me. So, I continue to lift my eyes to the hills from which cometh my help. "My help comes from the Lord, who made the heaven and the earth" (Psalm 121:2, NIV).

Chapter 3

Rejection in the workplace

For awhile, I worked at a hospital preparing meals. I loved my job and the people I worked with, but there was always an adversary in every bunch. There was a lady who hated me with a passion. She hated my very existence and would stop at nothing to make sure I knew it. Everyone else in my department knew it, too, which made me very uncomfortable.

It all started with an item placed in her area one day. Every day she talked *at* me through other people, sometimes trying to bump me while walking past. I would try to ignore it as long as I could before getting all stressed out.

The situation got so bad that I dreaded going to work. I started praying for her and myself. First, I asked the Lord to first forgive me, if I had done anything to cause the anger, malice, strife, bitterness, hatred, forgiveness and God only knew what else.

Next, I asked God to give me a forgiving heart towards her. Then I prayed Matthew 5:44, asking the Lord to teach me how to love my enemies, do good to them that hate me and persecute me. I asked the Lord to create in me a clean heart and renew the right spirit in me (Psalm 51:10). Then I asked the Lord to let this mind be in me that was also in Christ Jesus (Philippians 2:5). I prayed that the words of my mouth and the meditation of my heart would be acceptable in His sight, Oh Lord my strength and redeemer (Psalm 19:14).

Knowing that I would not be overcome with evil, but could overcome evil by doing good (Romans 12:12), I decided I would speak to her and was sure she would not speak back. I asked the Lord to open a door for me to talk to her. After praying many days for her, God, being faithful as always, set it up. I was going down to the basement on the elevator for stock. When the door opened, there she was, coming my way.

I asked her, "Whatever I did to cause you to feel the way you feel about me, could you please forgive me?"

She stood flat-footed and said, "Oh, no. I will not forgive you."

I felt so rejected and hurt because I was trying to make peace with her. I felt so disappointed because I had prayed so diligently for the both of us. I felt where I had tried to do good, evil was present.

So, I left it alone and walked away, and went back upstairs, knowing that I had done what was required of me. The Bible tells us, if you have offense against your brother, go to them. By doing so you could gain a brother if they listen (Matthew 18:15-17). The Bible also teaches us to forgive man his trespasses so that your heavenly Father will forgive you your trespasses (Matthew 6:14-15).

When you have done all you can, then remind yourself of Ephesians 6:13, NIV: "Therefore, take up the whole armor of God, that you may be able to withstand in the evil day, and having done all to stand." You will be able to stand on God's Word and He will make your enemy your footstool (Psalm 110:1).

Two hours later, I heard her call my name and she asked if I would come over to her workstation. Even though I feared what might happen or that she might make a scene, I did go.

She said, "Okay. I forgive you, but I choose not to deal with you."

I replied, "Okay. Fine. Thank you."

While we never became friends, from that point on we were cordial to each other.

One thing the Holy Spirit showed me was that it was not her attacking me but a spirit operating through her. The enemy was fighting against the Spirit of God that lives within me. I had to deal with it through prayer, not my flesh. I had to do what Jesus would do. Do good to those who do evil toward you. Vengeance is the Lord's. Be careful when you dislike a person. Do not try to turn everyone else against them. "Be not deceived; God is not mocked. Whatsoever a man soweth, that shall he also reap" (Galatians 6:7, KJV). This means that if you sow evil seed, evil will come your way. Whatever you do, be sure to seek and sow love, joy, peace, reconciliation, restoration, healing, and friendship.

Especially in the workplace, you never know whom you are blessing or who will be a blessing to you. The very person you reject could be your connection to your destiny. We must strive to live peacefully with all men (Romans 12:18).

Chapter 4

Rejection in the Kingdom or Body of Christ

Recently, while on high alert, and praying and fasting, I was inspired by the Holy Spirit to work on my book. Here is what I felt led to write.

There is no rejection or hurt like that which comes from the body of Christ. When rejection and hurt happens in the world, you expect it because the world doesn't know the God we serve. When you are hurt by the world through rejection, the Bible tells you to pray that their eyes would be enlightened.

We know that they are of the world and we are of Christ and have a relationship with God; we know that we're supposed to be *in* the world but not *of* this world. Second Corinthians 10:3 (NIV) says, "For though we live in the world, we do not wage war as the world does. "As the body of Christ, we cannot act like people in the world because the house of the Lord is supposed to be a house of prayer for all nations to be healed. God's house should be a healing place for everyone to come and celebrate what has happened throughout the week and a place of fellowship with one another. That's why rejection in the Body of Christ can hurt so much more.

Rejection in the Body of Christ is a spiritual wound that only God can heal because it is a deeper internal wound. The Bible says that offense will come but you have to forgive and stop talking about it to everyone except God. God can heal your heart so you won't go around spreading venom on everyone that hurt you. Sometimes we want everyone to join in our pity party, and before we know it we have sown discord and strife throughout the Body of Christ. Hurting people hurt others because they are looking for someone to hurt and feel the pain that is in their heart.

When you have a headache, you can take an aspirin to ease the pain. When you have a toothache, you can put some medicine on the tooth to numb the pain. When you have a backache, you use a rub to soothe the pain. When your feet hurt, you can soak them in Epsom Salts to relieve the pain.

But when your heart aches, there's nothing you can do but take it to God. You are going to need the Lord to heal the brokenness in your heart. The Lord God is your physician and the Lord God that heals you says, "Beloved, above all things, I wish for you to prosper and be in health even as your soul prospers" (3 John 2, NIV).

When your heart is hurting from the pain of rejection, take it to the Lord, not your neighbor or other people. Sometimes, instead of praying it through, people spread gossip and slander. If you are to stand in the midst of rejection and not give up or give in, you need to give it to God. Cry out for your healing. Ask God to do heart surgery to take away the pain, the bruises, the very residue and the core of the hurt. It may take going to God more than once, but continue to ask for forgiveness and continue to *choose* to forgive.

Forgiveness is a choice, because God gave us free will

and we are free will moral agents. We can choose to forgive and let go of those things that so easily hinder us or hold us down. Unforgiveness holds us back in our prayer life, ministries, relationships, successes, and other areas of our lives.

Do not give others that kind of power over your life. It will hold you back while others go on with their lives. Being bound by unforgiveness steals your joy, peace, and happiness, and makes you lose focus on what God wants you to do. Don't let others affect the purpose that God has for you. Don't allow your growth and maturity in Christ to stagnate!

Chapter 5

What Does the Bible Say About Rejection?

You have to know that there is a God who sits high, but He is always looking low. God said to cast all your cares upon Him for He cares for you (1 Peter 5:7). In your walk with Christ, as you take a stand for Him and righteousness, you are going to face rejection. Remember, Jesus was hated and rejected; even Judas, who walked with Christ, betrayed Him.

In this life, you're going to have Judases that will walk with you. You are going to have to put on the whole armor of God to be able to endure the wiles of the enemy and love your Judases anyway.

The second greatest commandment is to love thy neighbor as yourself (Matthew 22:39). We are also to love one another as Jesus has loved us. In the Parable of the Good Samaritan, we read:

> "On one occasion an expert in the law stood up to test Jesus. "Teacher," he asked, "what

must I do to inherit eternal life?"

"What is written in the Law?" he replied. "How do you read it?"

He answered, "'Love the Lord your God with all your heart and with all your soul and with all your strength and with all your mind'; and, 'Love your neighbor as yourself.'"

"You have answered correctly," Jesus replied. "Do this and you will live."

(Luke 10: 25-28, NIV)

In this walk, there are also going to be some Peters and "Judas's" along the way who will deny you. But the Bible tells us count it all joy when we fall into various temptations. Temptations are meant to try your faith and develop patience in you, and you are to let patience have its perfect work, so that you lack nothing (see James 1:4-8).

As well, keep in mind what Jesus said: "You have heard that it was said, 'Love your neighbor and hate your enemy.' But I tell you, love your enemies and pray for those who persecute you, that you may be children of your Father in heaven" (Matthew 5:43-45, NIV). And always remember the Apostle Paul's words: "Do not take revenge, my dear friends, but leave room for God's wrath, for it is written: 'It is mine to avenge; I will repay,' says the Lord. On the contrary: 'If your enemy is hungry, feed him; if he is thirsty, give him something to drink. In doing this, you will heap burning coals on his head.' Do not be overcome by evil, but overcome evil with good" (Romans 12:19-21, NIV).

Chapter 6

How to Deal with Rejection

If there's anything I know about prayer it is that supplication works. When the Bible says, "Pray without ceasing" (1 Thessalonians 5:16), that is what you have to do to stand in the midst of rejection. You have to cry out to God and give Him all your pain and disappointment, and allow Him to set you free. God will bring people into your life that will encourage you to go through healing and deliverance.

When you think you are healed from all the pain and hurt, God will reveal to you any unclean and unhealthy spirits that may still be manifesting in your heart. He will show you the core of your hurt and soul, in order for you to begin the cleansing process by renouncing, binding, rebuking, and releasing those things that have kept you in bondage. These are the things you may not have dealt with, which are the root causes of the rejection that manifest in your heart. People are still in ministries, preaching, teaching, laying hands, and passing on these things in the Body of Christ.

We need healing from our wounds, brokenness, hurt, pain, and unforgiveness in order to grow. We should seek

God every day and allow Him to work in us to become better preachers, teachers, intercessors, mentors and friends. We must grow spiritually to become a blessing to others that do not know His goodness.

2 Chronicles 7:14, KJV, says, "If my people which are called by my name will humble themselves and pray and seek my face turn from their wickedness then I will hear from heaven. I will forgive them of their sins and heal their land."

You have to move out of the way and let God work in your life to bring about change.

I had to be separated for a period of time from family, friends, and loved ones in order to get my healing. People will sometimes turn a blind eye to the work God has done in your life. Don't worry! This may be what *they* need to see the work God is doing, and to let Him work in their lives. You must let the Holy Spirit and the Word heal you.

I got to the point where I had to let the Holy Spirit reveal to me what I had to do to stop hurting. One thing that was evident: I had to remove me, myself, and I out of the way, and step back and "let go and let God." I know it seems hard to step back from that person that hurt you, but I encourage you, if you can just pray, worship, cry out, and praise your creator God and call on Him for help, He will be your help in time of trouble (Psalm 46:10).

Always remember the words Jesus spoke in John 14:27 (NIV): "Peace I leave with you; my peace I give you. I do not give to you as the world gives. Do not let your hearts be troubled and do not be afraid."

Let Christ love you through your pain. Go through healing and deliverance with a ministry or person you trust. Then seek God's face, invite and welcome the Holy Spirit in daily, and pray in your heavenly language *daily*, so the Holy Spirit can revive and heal you. The Holy Spirit can then burn up that hurt and those things that are unlike God.

Note: If you are not filled with the Holy Spirit with

the evidence of speaking in tongues, I encourage you to seek this gift: it is truly powerful! Acts 1:8, KJV, says, "But you will receive power when the Holy Spirit comes on you; and you will be my witnesses in Jerusalem, and in all Judea and Samaria, and to the ends of the earth." Keep in mind the words of Jesus:

> Ask and it will be given to you; seek and you will find; knock and the door will be opened to you. For everyone who asks receives; the one who seeks finds; and to the one who knocks, the door will be opened. "Which of you, if your son asks for bread, will give him a stone? Or if he asks for a fish, will give him a snake? If you, then, though you are evil, know how to give good gifts to your children, how much more will your Father in heaven give good gifts to those who ask him!

Matthew 7:7-11, NIV

I encourage you to seek after God's power to overcome!

Chapter 7

How to Stand in the Midst of Rejection

You must know who you are instead of how people see you. You have to know that you are fearfully and wonderfully made.

"I praise you because I am fearfully and wonderfully made; your works are wonderful, I know that full well" (Psalms 139:14, NIV).

"The Lord will make you the head and not the tail; you shall be above only and not be beneath; if you heed the commandments of the Lord your God, which I command you this day, and are careful to observe them" (Deuteronomy 28:13, NKJV).

"For I know the thoughts that I think toward you, says the Lord, thoughts of peace and not of evil, to give you a future and a hope" (Jeremiah 29:11, NKJV).

Do you see? It's not what people think about you; it's what God thinks and says about you. You are responsible for how you feel about others; that's what you will be held accountable for and how you treat others. You are to take on the attitude of Jesus and ask yourself, "What would Jesus do?"

When people rejected Him and said all manner of evil against Him, He prayed for those who mistreated Him. Jesus said, "But if you do not forgive men their trespasses, neither will your Father forgive your trespasses" Matthew 6:15 (NKJV). To forgive means to let go of any anger and desire to punish someone who has wronged you. We are to have mercy as God has mercy on us. The word "trespass" means stepping over a boundary by disobeying a law or doing wrong. You might not feel like you want to let things go, especially if someone is in your face, but the Word of God says we must forgive.

Chapter 8

Who Can Better Identify Rejection than Christ?

Who can better be an example of someone who faced complete rejection than Christ Himself? Jesus is the only one who did nothing wrong from the very beginning to the end of time, leading by example, and teaching us that we can handle rejection in the midst of a storm. We are not to give up or give in; it's our duty to endure like good soldiers, whatever we are going through.

We say that we want to do the will of the Father which is in heaven (Matthew 7:21). But, consider that Jesus did nothing wrong. He was the Son of God the Father. He went around doing good, feeding people, healing people, loving people, and casting out demons. Jesus can tell you better than I can what it feels like to be tormented by the pain that comes from being rejected. He was rejected in His hometown of Nazareth, His own people, and those who once said they loved Him. When Jesus entered the Samaritan Village, He was not welcome. He was rejected in Jerusalem by the people and the Jewish leadership.

Jesus was rejected by two of His disciples: Peter who rejected Him three times, and Judas who betrayed Him (see John 18:13-27). Judas' betrayal caused Jesus to be wrongfully accused and persecuted. He was taken from judgement hall to judgement hall where He was beaten, scourged (whipped), spit upon, and slapped. People threw stones at Him, and the Roman soldiers put a crown of thorns on His head. He was forced to carry His own cross after His body had been torn to shreds. They pierced His hands and feet, and gave Him vinegar to drink. He was mocked the entire time by the people who, a week earlier, had been cheering His arrival in Jerusalem. Yet, He showed love by forgiving His malefactors, the people who had done all these things to Him because they did not know what they were doing. Jesus also forgave the thief who repented and was crucified to the right of Him; He suffered all things for our sake.

However, three days after his crucifixion, He rose from the dead with all power! But that was not the end of His story. Jesus did that so that we may have life. He did not come into the world to condemn us (John 3:16-17). Instead, "I have come that they may have life, and that they may have *it* more abundantly" (John 10:10, NIV).

Jesus had to go away, to leave this earth, in order for the promise to be fulfilled. However, He sent a Helper, the Holy Ghost, who would lead and guide us and teach all truth (John 14:26).

Thank you, Holy Spirit, for being the third Godhead of the Trinity. It is because of You that people are drawn into a relationship with our Heavenly Father.

Jesus' desire for all of us is to be filled with the Holy Spirit and be baptized with the fire of the Holy Ghost! The Holy Ghost gives us the power to be effective witnesses, and to lay hands on people to cast out demons and heal the sick.

Chapter 9

A Word from the Lord

I received this word from the Lord concerning this book:

"Be quick to hear, slow to speak, and slow to anger; for the wrath of man worketh not the righteousness of God (James 1:19). My people need to hear your story, and as they read and mediate on this book, they, too, will be healed, delivered, and set free. The Body of Christ is hurting, and I have given you some of the keys to ease the pain. My daughter, will you allow Me to heal my people through what I have given you?

"My daughter, my friend, and servant, your latter days will be your greater days. As you see, I did not allow you to be rejected or wounded without my knowledge.

"The enemy desires you to be shredded like wheat, but I have prayed for you. You will walk in the destiny and purpose I have ordained you to walk in. My daughter, get ready; this is your season ... walk in it. Watch, pray, and obey, and I will show you evidence of your prayers. 'The effectual fervent prayer of a righteous man availeth much' (James 5:16). So stand and see the salvation of the Lord. 'I know the thoughts I think towards you, says the Lord, thoughts of peace and not of evil to give an expected end' (Jeremiah 29:11).

"My daughter, friend, and servant, I will tell you again, your latter days will be your greater days. I did not allow you to go through the pain of rejection, of being wounded, to hurt you but to heal you and others as you write this book. People will be healed, delivered, and set free as they read these pages."

To my readers, please say this prayer:

Father, thank you for the mountain that you have removed from my life … and those you will continue to remove from my life. Thank you for walking me through the valleys and for walking me through the valleys that will come. Thank you for giving me the grace to forgive every person, every hurt, wound, and source of rejection. I continue to forgive every person who has hurt, wounded, or rejected me; every person who invaded my privacy and places I experienced rejection and hurt. I choose to forgive everyone and anything that has caused me hurt and rejection, in the name of Jesus. I wash myself in the blood of Jesus, the blood that cleanses me from all sin and unrighteousness.

Father, shine Your light on every area of bitterness, hatred, jealousy, unforgiveness, oppression, depression, thoughts of suicide, feeling un-loved, and rejected. I decree and declare that I give the Holy Spirit permission to take everything that is wrong in my life, and make me whole; make the crooked road straight in the mighty and miraculous name of (Yeshua) Jesus! Amen, and thank you Father.

Closing Prayer

Father,

I pray that all who read this book will be healed, delivered and set free by the power of Your Holy Spirit—spiritually, emotionally and physically.

I bind and rebuke all spirits of rejection that have caused hurt, disappointment, low self-esteem, unforgiveness, bitterness, and hatred.

I ask that You help everyone choose to forgive, just like You have forgiven them, and release them from every yoke, stronghold or bondage.

I proclaim Jesus' words in John 8:32 (NIV): "Therefore if the Son makes you free, you shall be free indeed."

In Jesus' name, amen!

Heartfelt Words from My Children

From my son, DeAndre Javon.

I just want to say thank you for being a real mother through tough times, rejection, trials, and tribulations. You are the true definition of a strong black woman. I know what it is like being rejected and judged by loved ones and so-called friends. It's not an easy pill to swallow, but I have watched you do it over and over and still show love. Rejection, I have to say has done nothing but made our family even stronger and made us push harder to succeed. Yes, it hurt but has also been a blessing, because at the end of the day you find out how to cherish genuine love and loyalty, which is priceless.

From my son, Claude LeVar.

Momma I remember when you first told me how Christ, through the Holy Spirit was dealing with you about your book. So, you told me one night when we were sitting in your kitchen on Edmore Street, "Var guess what I wrote some of my book, would you like to read it?" I said yes. But mom, I also dealt with rejection growing up and so I can relate. I love you Momma and may God bless you and your readers.

From my daughter, Tiffany Michelle.

Kingdom blessing and all praises be unto our Lord and Savior Jesus Christ. I am so excited and thankful to the Holy Spirit in moving on my mom to write a book, *How To Stand in the Mist of Rejection*. It will be life changing, not just to a certain group of people, but this book will be a blessing to the nations, whether you are a part of the Body of Christ or not. Everyone is experiencing rejection in some form or another. But what we lack is the antidote on how to overcome the spirit of rejection, and this book simply speaks of tools and strategies as well as testimonies on how the Holy Spirit dealt with my mom in overcoming the spirit of rejection effectively. And I pray that whoever reads this book that the Hoy Spirit will not just touch but deliver them from strongholds, unforgiveness, bitterness, resentment, and other spirits that are caused by rejection, and bring total healing and deliverance in the mind, heart, body, and soul.

From my son, Steven Martez.

I am honored that my mother has given me this opportunity to express my love for her in her book. She has my full support and understanding of her journey and testimony as it pertains to rejection. I can relate to the many different times in my life where I experienced rejection from friends, family, and relationships with women I was in love with, but the feelings were not mutual for them as it was for me. As I look back at myself, rejection was one of the most difficult things I (like my mother) had to overcome. I dealt with low self-esteem as if I did not belong, look good enough, or as if I was not smart enough. To God's glory, and because of a praying, loving mother, and anyone who had anything to do with my growth, I have triumphed over the years. Although, I was young when a lot of what my mother was going through was happening, I was a witness to some of the rejection she went through, and the emotional roller coaster and the toll it took on her. The Word of God, prayers, healing, deliverance, and her faith in God are what changed and strengthen her. I love my mother so much and thank God for her accepting Christ in her life, and helping to touch and change the lives of others through the help of the Holy Spirit.

About the Author

Elder Gloria G. Duff

Born and raised in Montgomery, Alabama, I attended Lowndes County Training School until age eleven. My mother then migrated to Michigan in 1966 with our family, and I followed in 1968. I attended Keating Elementary School, then proceeded to Foch Jr. High, before graduating from Southeastern High School. Years later, I graduated from Dorsey Business School. I also attend Goliath Culinary School.

I received salvation and was baptized at a young age and subsequently filled with the Holy Ghost. I attended Ministry School under the leadership of Bishop Michael Jones and Elder Ruby Gardner, and was licensed as a Minister and later ordained as an Elder in 2008. Later, I served as the Lead Intercessor at the Fountain of Truth Christian Center for approximately five years, until I transitioned to help serve Pastor Morris and Patricia Hampton at New Christian Missionary Baptist Church. I now attend Evangel Christian Church in Roseville, MI, under the leadership of the late Bishop Jerry and my senior pastor, Dr. Sherill Piscopo, where I serve on different ministry teams (Intercessory Prayer Team and Women of Vision Core

Team), and I serve as the lead facilitator for the Adult Sunday School. I have served in *Heart to Heart Ministries* and *Purity in Christ* where we mentored young ladies for several years under the leadership of Dr. Sharon Smith.

God birthed *100 Women and Men at the Water Prayer Ministry* in 2008, and He changed the name to *Gathering of the Intercessors* and *Gloria Duff Ministries* in 2020. I am also the business owner of "Honey Bunch II" baking and drop off catering. My passion is cooking, which I have 30 years of experience. And now here I am an author. My book titled *How to Stand in the Midst of Rejection* was a God journey and I'm so grateful to share it with the world!

If you would like to contact me, feel free to do so at: glorialisteenduff@yahoo.com

www.ingramcontent.com/pod-product-compliance
Lightning Source LLC
Chambersburg PA
CBHW061805070526
44586CB00023B/2721